"*A Different Home* transported me back to the time when, at the age of 7 or 8, I was dropped off with total strangers... They changed my life in a positive way, for which I am grateful, though much of my anxiety could have been relieved had they been able to read this book with me."

—Rhonda Sciortino, former foster child and author of *Succeed Because of What You've Been Through*

* * * * *

"The depth of empathy running through the story is heartfelt. I could hear, smell and feel the little one all the way through. This book will surely comfort and go some way to allay the very real fears that run through you as a child when being placed in the care system."

—Jenny Molloy, Looked After Children Adviser and Trainer, and author of *Hackney Child* written as Hope Daniels

* * * * *

"Accurate, honest, warm and a great resource for parents and professionals."

—Dr. Sue Cornbluth, Psychologist, National Expert in Foster Care/Adoption and Trauma, USA

for children

Adopted Like Me
My Book of Adopted Heroes
Ann Angel
Illustrated by Marc Thomas
ISBN 978 1 84905 935 0
eISBN 978 0 85700 740 7

Ladybird's Remarkable Relaxation
How children (and frogs, dogs, flamingos and dragons) can use yoga
relaxation to help deal with stress, grief, bullying and lack of confidence
Michael Chissick
Illustrated by Sarah Peacock
ISBN 978 1 84819 146 4
eISBN 978 0 85701 112 1

Frog's Breathtaking Speech
How Children (and Frogs) Can Use Yoga Breathing
to Deal with Anxiety, Anger and Tension
Michael Chissick
Illustrated by Sarah Peacock
ISBN 978 1 78775 613 7
eISBN 978 0 85701 074 2

for foster parents

The Foster Parenting Manual
A Practical Guide to Creating a Loving, Safe and Stable Home
Dr. John DeGarmo
Foreword by Mary Perdue
ISBN 978 1 84905 956 5
eISBN 978 0 85700 795 7

Foster Parenting Step-by-Step
How to Nurture the Traumatized Child and Overcome Conflict
Dr. Kalyani Gopal
Foreword by Irene Clements
ISBN 978 1 84905 937 4
eISBN 978 0 85700 751 3

Creating Loving Attachments
Parenting with PACE to Nurture Confidence
and Security in the Troubled Child
Kim S. Golding and Daniel A. Hughes
ISBN 978 1 84905 227 6
eISBN 978 0 85700 470 3

A DIFFERENT HOME

A New Foster Child's Story

John DeGarmo and Kelly DeGarmo
Illustrated by Norma Jeanne Trammell

Jessica Kingsley Publishers
London and Philadelphia

First edition published in hardback in Great Britain
in 2014 by Jessica Kingsley Publishers

This paperback edition published in Great Britain
in 2021 by Jessica Kingsley Publishers

An Hachette Company

1

A CIP catalogue record for this title is available from
the British Library and the Library of Congress

ISBN 978 1 83997 091 7
eISBN 978 0 85700 897 8

Printed and bound in the United Kingdom by Ashford Colour Press Ltd

Jessica Kingsley Publishers' policy is to use papers that are natural,
renewable and recyclable products and made from wood grown in
sustainable forests. The logging and manufacturing processes are expected
to conform to the environmental regulations of the country of origin.

Jessica Kingsley Publishers
Carmelite House
50 Victoria Embankment
London EC4Y 0DZ

www.jkp.com

For Patti Sue and Caitlen, who first changed my family

One day I was at school in Mrs. Miller's class. It's a nice class, and it is lots of fun. Mrs. Miller is really friendly. I like school a lot.

Then, a strange lady came into the class. She talked to Mrs. Miller. They kept staring at me, and Mrs. Miller looked a little worried. The strange lady walked over to my desk and asked me to come to the office with her. She told me her name was Kathy. She smiled at me, and she smelled really good.

I thought I was in trouble. Kathy told me that
everything would be okay now. But I thought
everything was okay already. Then, I started to
get scared.

"Is everything okay?" I asked her. "Yes, Jessie, it is," Kathy said. She said I wouldn't be going home today. Kathy told me that my mommy was a little sick, and that she had to get better before I could go back home. But I wanted to go home. Instead, I had to sit in the office. I was scared.

The people in the office told me that somebody else was going to come and pick me up. I had to wait a long time. I watched my friends get on the bus to go home. I wanted to go home too.

Then, Kathy came back and brought another lady and man with her. "Hi Jessie, this is Debbie and Jim," Kathy said. She told me I was going to go to a different home, that I was going home with them. But they were strangers. I wanted my mommy.

Debbie knelt down and took my hand and said hello. She told me that she would take me home and that I could have a snack when I got there. I wanted a snack, but I didn't want to go with her to her house. I started to cry.

The man talked with Kathy for a long time,
and then he and Debbie signed a lot of papers.
Then he came over to me and ruffled my hair.
"Hi Jessie, my name is Jim. Let's go home." He
smiled a lot, and took me by the hand. I wanted
to go home to my mommy.

We drove to a house. It was bigger than mine,
and nice. I still liked mine better, though.
There were a bunch of older kids in the house.
They were all happy to see me. They laughed,
and played, and were noisy. I wasn't happy to
be there.

Debbie and Jim kept telling me that everything would be okay. I just wanted to go home.

Their house was warm, and before we went
to bed everybody had a cup of hot chocolate
and seven marshmallows. We even had some
homemade chocolate chip cookies. I didn't
tell them that I liked the hot chocolate and
cookies…but I did. I still liked my house
better, though.

I got to sleep in my very own bed, all by myself. I'd never done that before. The sheets smelled good. I was so scared, though. I cried and cried and cried for my mommy.

Debbie came into the room and read me a story. Then she said that everything was going to be okay, and that my mommy was getting the help she needed. I didn't think it would ever be okay, though.

When I woke up the next morning, I could smell something yummy. I was hungry, but I was too afraid to go downstairs. I didn't remember where the kitchen was, and I didn't know whether I was allowed to go downstairs or not.

I didn't know whether the breakfast I could
smell was going to be for me, so I snuck into the
big boy's bedroom, took his big bag of candy,
and hid it under my pillow for later. When I
turned around the big boy was right there. He
said, "Good morning, I just came to get you for

breakfast. Ready?" He pretended not to see the candy, but I knew he did.

I was so hungry, and it smelled so good. I went downstairs. There was a lot of food. Everybody had a plate.

I didn't want to eat their food, but I was hungry. I'd never smelled breakfast like this. There were blueberry pancakes, bacon, eggs, and orange juice. It was going to be the best breakfast I'd ever had.

Debbie and Jim sat at the table, and so did the other kids. There was no yelling or fighting, and no one getting slapped on the hand, like at my house. It was very different.

After breakfast, it was time to get dressed and get ready for school. I didn't have any of my clothes, but they had new clothes for me. The clothes felt stiff and uncomfortable, but smelled like new. I missed my old clothes, but I liked these new ones too.

Soon, it was time to go to school. I didn't have to wait outside to catch the bus. Instead, Debbie drove us all to school in a big car. I was happy to be back at school because I saw Mrs. Miller, and I knew her rules.

I thought everything would be okay after school, and I'd be going back home to my mommy, but Debbie came to pick me up again. When I saw her, my tummy felt really sick and I started to cry. I wanted to go home to my house. I wanted to be with my mommy, not somebody else's mommy.

That night, I asked Debbie where my mommy was, and said that I wanted to see her. I told her I wanted to go home. "Did I do something wrong? Is my mommy mad at me?" I asked. "Oh no, Jessie, you didn't do anything wrong at all. Your mommy loves you very much. She just needs to work on a few things," Debbie said. I didn't know what kind of things my mommy needed to work on.

"We just don't know when she will get better, so we don't know when you can go home, sweetheart. In the meantime, will you stay with us? We'd really like you to stay with our family for a while.

I know it's hard, sweetie, and it's okay to be scared. As your foster parents, we will try to help make it a little easier for you and will take care of you."

Jim came in and sat next to Debbie. He put his arm around her, and smiled at me. "That's right, Jessie, we want to help you. We care about you, and will make sure that you are okay while you're living with us."

Debbie and Jim were really nice, and I liked them. I didn't want to hurt their feelings and tell them that I didn't want to be there, so I didn't say anything.

On Saturday, we didn't go to school. I missed
Mrs. Miller, but it was okay. Debbie and Jim's
kids were nice to me, and I did like to play with
them. They even let me play with their toys.

After lunch, we went to a park. Debbie and Jim brought a picnic for all of us. I'd never had a picnic before. There was so much food! Then, we played Frisbee, and played on the swing.

Then, we all went to have ice cream. I tried
really hard not to smile that day, because I
wanted them to know that I missed my mommy.
But I did smile when they said I could choose
my own ice cream flavor.

When we got back to their home, we had
dinner, and then it was time for bed. Debbie
and Jim both read me a story in bed, and then
gave me a kiss on the cheek.

This isn't my family, it's my foster family, but I do like them. And this home isn't my home, it's a different home, but it's okay for now. Until my mommy gets her stuff worked out, I will stay and live here with Debbie, Jim, and their own kids. And that's okay, too.

Afterword
Advice for Foster Parents
When a Foster Child Arrives
in Your Home

Imagine being seven years old. Without warning, you are suddenly taken away from your mother, your father, your pets, your bedroom, your stuffed animals, your home, your grandparents, your aunts and uncles, your cousins, your neighbors, your friends, your teacher, your school; everything that is familiar to you. You are thrust into a different home against your will—a strange home with strange people—and told that this is your new home, that this is your new family. As a seven-year-old child, how would you react?

For foster children the world over, placement into a new home is a frightening experience. So many questions fill their minds. Questions such as, "Did I do anything wrong?" "When can I go home?" "Will I ever see my family again?" "Who are these people that I am living with?" These are just a few of the many questions that foster children ask. In this book, Jessie has many questions, is scared, and just wants to go home. Like Jessie, most children entering foster care will want their mother and father back. After all, these people have been the most important people in her life. Along with this, she has lost her familiar pattern of living, her home, her friends, and all that made up her own personal world. Although it is impossible to predict how she will react when she first meets you, it is important that you approach this time with caution and care. A foster child's first few days in a new home are often pivotal for the health and wellbeing of all involved.

When Jessie's foster parents, Debbie and Jim, answer her questions and tell her it is okay to be scared, Jessie starts to feel a little better about her new foster home. By the end of the story, Jessie feels a little better about the whole situation—the family she is with, and the different home she is now living in.

We wrote this book for foster parents to read to a foster child upon placement into their home. Foster children often experience a myriad of emotions when they are first placed into a foster home. Powerful emotions of loss, grief, sorrow, confusion, and even fear may quickly overwhelm a foster child during this time of transition. As a result, a foster home can quickly descend into a state of turmoil, leading to a very unhealthy environment. Foster parents need to be prepared to meet the challenges raised by these emotions as they strive to make their foster child's transition a little less stressful. We hope that this book will help to start conversations—to explore and answer important questions, such as "Why am I here?" "What happened?" "What are foster parents?" "Will I go home soon?" We also hope that the book will provide foster parents with a sense of what it is like to be a foster child entering foster care.

As experienced foster carers, below are some tips for welcoming a new foster child into your home, which we have found helpful over the years.

The first impression you create with your foster child will be vitally important as it is likely to impact how the next few days and weeks will transpire. She will probably not be a sweet little child who rushes into your waiting arms, laughing delightedly. It is highly likely that the foster child entering care will be scared and frightened, full of anxiety. She may have left her family only moments ago, to suddenly be told that you are her family for the time being. She will be full of questions, as emotions swirl within her. Although it is impossible to predict how she will react when she first meets you, approach this time with caution and care.

When the caseworker or social worker pulls into your driveway, go out to the car and welcome the caseworker and the child. Introduce yourself and your family, with a warm smile and soft voice. It's a good idea to tell your foster child who you are and explain the role you will now play in her life at the outset, as she may not understand the foster care system, or what foster parents do. Allow your foster child to call you by your first names if you feel comfortable with this, or by whatever name she feels comfortable calling you (avoid asking her to call you Mom or Dad).

A child entering foster care may not react to new foster parents right away, and may be in a state of shock. As you help her inside with her possessions, take her by the hand (if a young child) or place a soft hand upon her shoulder. Actions like these can be reassuring that all will be okay, and that she is in a safe and caring home. Hugs or kisses will be too much, and are likely to embarrass, hurt, or even threaten the child.

Show her where she will sleep, and where her clothes will be kept. Have a nightlight already on in her bedroom if the room is dark. Ask whether she is hungry, and offer her some food. If she doesn't want any food, do not insist upon it. She will eat when she is ready and hungry.

If you have to sign any paperwork for a social worker or caseworker, try to do this away from the child. This is a good time for your foster child to eat, or to be alone in her new room. If you have children of your own, this may also be a good time for them to engage in some sort of play with their new foster sibling. Your foster child will likely be overwhelmed with the situation, so it is important that you make sure your home is as peaceful and quiet as possible. Allow her to have some personal space and alone time.

If it is late at night, do not insist that she goes to bed immediately. After all, she will probably need some time to reflect on the day's events, and sleep may be difficult to come by as she is in a strange bed, in a strange home. Sadly, it is not uncommon for newly placed foster children to cry themselves to sleep during the first few nights. Do not be surprised if this happens. She may be scared and lonely. Let her know that you understand how difficult it is for her, and that her tears are normal and all right. Read a bedtime story to her each night; place a nightlight not only in her room, but in the nearby bathroom as well. Let her know that she can get up in the night and use the bathroom whenever she needs to. With a few preparations, and a lot of comfort and understanding, you can help to make your foster child's transition a little easier.

We hope that you find this book helpful. For more information and resources about foster parenting, do get in touch via John's website (http://drjohndegarmofostercare.weebly.com). John is also the author of *The Foster Parenting Manual: A Practical Guide to Creating a Loving, Safe and Stable Home* (Jessica Kingsley Publishers)—a guide written to provide proven, friendly advice for novice and experienced parents alike.